I'll Be Running for President ..
.. will you join me???

John J Larkin

DEDICATION

.. dedicated to GrandBaby, Charlie, who we were blessed with in January 2011 ..

.. to his cousin who will join us November 2012 ..

.. to both sets of their parents ..

.. and really .. to all posterity ..

May God continue to bless us, all ..

.. and .. America!!!

CONTENTS

<u>Foreword</u>

As I was preparing this book (and learning a lot about writing books and publishing), one of my dear friends kept after me almost daily checking on its progress.

As you'll be able to tell as you read the following pages, the book was prompted by all that was going on in the days ahead of, and the lead-up to, the national elections in November of 2012.

My friend is an experienced marketer and was driven by the window of opportunity for the book that would be present prior to the elections; and while it's true that some may find this work more significant during that period of time, the truth is, the books message is somewhat timeless.

Our Country became the envy of the world because of the outcomes of a divinely inspired guide that was put together for us at the birth of our Nation.

Our "enviable" position will return to our Nation in larger measures when we return to the "guide" that propelled it towards its greatness – whenever that happens.

Whether in the elections in 2012 or sometime afterward ..
we must get back to it!

<u>Let's pray for soon</u>!!!

A Country in Trouble

Our Country is being propelled towards catastrophic trouble of all sorts and our leaders (and many of those proposing to be our leaders) are prancing about like a litter of week old barking puppies. Who's going to get their spot at the government teat first and be able to stay there the longest?

Our economy is sliding into ruinous destinations – insolvency even. Our borders are unsecured and we're being invaded by all sorts of unsavory characters. Our economic position in the world is becoming more and more questionable by the day. Our citizenry is more visibly divided than ever before. Our military is stretched thin across the globe and becoming dangerously weakened by political financial "cuts". And here at home, a measurable and growing air of significant discomfort and palpable tension is apparent.

We, indeed, are a Country in trouble!

And .. there doesn't seem to be a lasting and effective resolution for our challenges at hand or one even close.

Politicians are playing politics and appear to be racing to show their adeptness at political gymnastics. Talking heads are spewing their expert insights and opinions eagerly; and most frequently, contrary to fact or common sense. And .. the media continues to spew the most recent liberal talking points and misleading propaganda.

People outside of this country must be watching with complete aghast as the greatest, most prosperous, and most free country in the entire world seemingly self destructs.

Where is the answer to our dilemmas?

Where is that "magic formula" that will help us out of our troubles?

Does such an answer .. such a "magic formula" exist?

When and how can we implement this resolution to our difficulties?

And .. how will we go about it?

<u>The truth is such a "magic formula" does exist!</u>

And .. it's available to us.

Literally, at our very fingertips.

If executed with a cautious, honest and sincere effort, this formula will extract us from our difficulties and challenges and propel us back into a position of peace, prosperity, and global distinction!

I can say this with great confidence because the formula's outcomes have done exactly that before in this great Country's history!

As a person who's going to "be running for President" – with you hopefully – you can be very assured that I'll do everything I can to make sure this formula gets introduced and applied.

We want this Country to be lifted up from its death spiral!

We want this Country to continue to succeed and grow!

And, I believe, we'll have a tremendous amount of support in reviving this formula and reinstituting it as a routine way of doing business (again) here in the United States of America. Especially, once we revisit it and again experience the benefits of the plan.

If, for some reason, we're unsuccessful with our mission, I fear that our Republic .. our Country .. the United States of America .. may continue to slide uncontrollably downward into that "thousand years of darkness" that we've been warned of.

Not only just the United States .. but the world may join us in that darkness!

God willing .. for our sake and for the sake of all posterity .. we must succeed in our mission!!!

So yes .. I'll be running for President ..

.. and hoping you'll join me!

Okay - So Why You? Why Us – Why You and Me?

Well .. I don't know about you; but I **love** America!!!

I love our Country and **all** it represents! I love our way of life and culture! I love our citizenry. I love our military! I love our flag! I still tear up hearing our National Anthem and knowing the story of its origins! I love our history and our journey!

Simply put .. I Love America!!!

.. and I'm believing you do, too!

Furthermore, I look for opportunity to proudly herald our Country to others .. not to apologize for it or denigrate it!

I can recognize and am aware of our missteps – I am a realist and know perfection is not the norm on this planet; but I would always be very mindful of the greatness of this Country and its people.

I would always remember the tremendous compassion this Country has always shown and extended to the world.

I'm very aware of the huge amounts of innovation and conveniences this Country has brought forward and given to the world.

With humble admiration, I'm also very conscious of how much, and how often, this Country has brought aid of all sorts to those in trouble and suffering.

And .. I wouldn't be hesitant to remind others of it, either.

Humbly so; but indeed very mindful of the graciousness of a Loving God who has blessed America with so many wonderful and helpful gifts to share, indeed, with the world.

As well, I have a deep devotion to God, to God and Country, and to others – to be of good service.

I come from a long line of decorated veterans; and I myself am a veteran of the United States Coast Guard.

I believe with all my heart, and life if necessary, that the United States of America with all its goodness and merit must be safeguarded and preserved for this generation and for all those yet to come.

The US of A needs to be here for not only we Americans; but for all, as a hopeful example and illuminating beacon of liberty and freedom to the world.

I'm very steadfast in my belief that God has blessed and favored America immensely; and that He will continue to as we invite and ask Him.

I believe, with absolute conviction, that America has been the grandest and greatest example of liberty and freedom the world has ever known; and for the sake of the world, must continue to be!

The truth is that we are a country in a decline. The truth is that it will take a very focused and energized effort to change that direction. But the truth is also, that we can do it.

We're Americans!

We're capable and good people!

We've experienced Liberty and Freedom!

We do need to get to work. We need a plan. We need leadership.

That's why I'll be running for President .. hopefully with you!

And .. just so that you know .. I was definitely born here!!!

Good old St. Paul, Minnesota - Midwest, USA

And in case there's any law abiding American citizens out there that need some proof of my legitimacy to run for office – which is certainly within their rights – I'd be happy to satisfy their concerns even if it meant producing my birth certificate. I'd probably even applaud their efforts and desire to safeguard the integrity of elections here in this Country and the Rule of Law.

And just so that you know, **everyone** in my family and in my circle of friends **is, and always has been, PROUD of this COUNTRY!!!**

And, I .. would be proud to be of service to you and my Country!!!

So, yes .. I'll be running for President; and I'm inviting you to join with me as well. Let's step to the plate and do what we can to come to the aid of our Country and begin to turn this ship-of-state around in a very meaningful fashion.

Our goal will not be to transform America, but to "refresh" and "restore" her.

To honor and safeguard her.

To help breathe a fresh breath of that precious "American Spirit" into her.

Join me as we embark to refresh and restore America!!!

Let's run.

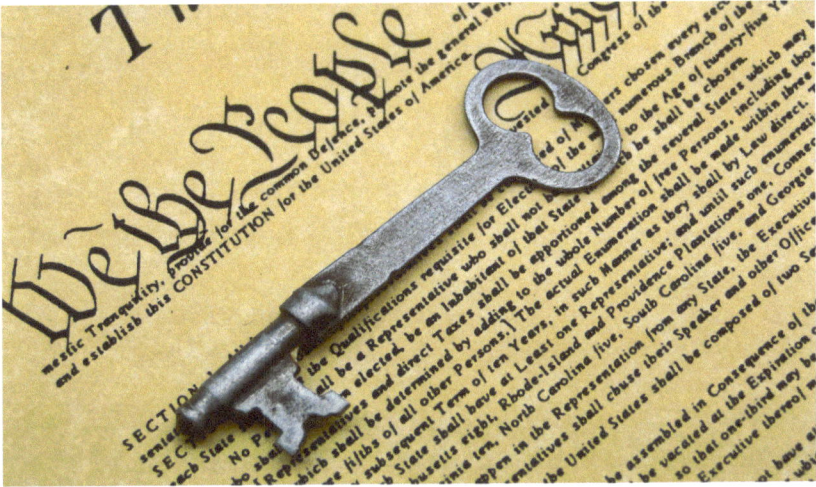

<u>Okay</u> .. <u>So Where to from Here?</u>

Great question!

First things, first.

We need to do some very sincere soul searching and ask ourselves if we are honestly committed to being part of the effort to help save and preserve our Country – the greatest and freest land in the history of the world.

I'm oftentimes reminded of the answer a little girl offered to the question, "what's meant by being 'committed' to something?"

God bless this little gal.

Her response to that question was, "I think being committed to something means ... to do it, or die."

How's that for "out of the mouths of babes"?

And, of course, her answer propels me to think of those fifty-six very brave and committed men who penned their names to our magnificent Declaration of Independence and started this greatest experiment in liberty and freedom.

They swore, "And for the support of this Declaration, with a firm reliance on the protection of Divine Providence, we mutually pledge to each other our Lives, our Fortunes, and our sacred Honor."

Those very courageous and committed men knew the King of England would want their heads!

Those courageous and committed men knew they, and their families, would be in an extremely dangerous position ... all so that people could live free someday!

How's that for commitment?

And to a man, not one turned their back on their pledge, spite of personal hardships and calamity to themselves and their families, including even, death for some.

Free people everywhere are in their debt!!!

We've yet to be asked to go to the lengths those fifty-six men went to, but would a citizen of today willingly offer to put their signature to a document declaring their freedom from whatever; knowing, they'd likely lose their fortunes, they and their family would be subject to vengeful tortures of all sorts, and all of them could lose their lives?

Thank God, as a rule, we've yet to be asked to go to those levels; but would we if called to?

How committed to the success and longevity of this grand country – this greatest place on earth are we?

What would we be willing to sacrifice? .. to put on the line?

Would I rise to "the call"; or, would I drop into my much more convenient comfort zone?

"Gosh .. will I have to miss "American Idol"?!?!?"

How committed to my Country am I?

What am I willing to sacrifice .. to put forth .. to do my part in securing the blessings and liberties I've enjoyed here in America for the generations yet to come?

Those are amongst the questions that should not go unanswered.

What am I giving back to my Country now? What am I doing, on a regular basis, to make sure our way of life stays intact and our Country even gets better?

Am I going to the City Council meetings? Am I staying on top of what's happening in my local schools and school board?

Am I paying attention to what's happening on the state and national levels?

Am I making sure our foundational values and principles are being honored and are intact? Do I even know what they are?

Am I willing to "run for President"?

Am I willing to do even a small part in helping make this country work?

Am I aware of the huge sacrifices that were made by Americans before me?

Am I truly grateful for all those sacrifices and for how well they have benefited me?

Like those fifty-six signers of our Declaration of Independence .. am I ready to "pledge to each other our Lives, our Fortunes, and our sacred Honor"?

I'm ready .. are you?

Let's run!

Sounds Like a Lot of Work!

Sounds like a big commitment!

Filtering and sifting through the insanity of what we have going on in this country today is a lot of work! A tremendous amount of work!

Staying on top of things is a big commitment. A commitment that must be undertaken; or, having to suffer the consequences of not.

The politicians are politicking. The talking heads are regurgitating the assortment of talking points. The media is working overtime to spin specific agendas and further their propaganda. Most all levels of academia have been poisoned with revisionary misinformation and ideologies that are against the American grain; and they are doing their very best to spread that poison to our young.

Who do we believe? What do we believe?

How about we start to put more belief in ourselves and our ability to know that when things don't seem to make sense .. they probably aren't sensible.

How about we remember there is no free lunch.

How about we recall that when it sounds too good to be true, that it usually isn't true.

Or, when they're urinating on our shoes, we don't let them convince us it's rain.

Nowadays, there is just too much technology and too much information available to us for us not to do a little research of our own and determine more of these things for ourselves. We don't need to continue to surrender our intelligence to people who have repeatedly demonstrated that their ideas and plans are wrong; and allow them to push us in very, very dangerous directions.

We're also extremely fortunate that there is a growing body of Americans that are no longer putting their faith in the fact that "if you heard it, or saw it, on the news .. it must be true!" They're not putting blind trust in the leaders who are placing us in destructive positions.

More and more, the louder voice of the American people is clamoring much like the people in the Aesop's fable, "The Emperor's New Clothes", ...

"Hey, Mr. Emperor, .. You have no clothes on! You are naked!"

The old conviction that "you can't fight city hall" is rapidly losing its bite .. its grip. Not only can we "fight city hall" .. confused, misguided, corrupt, self-serving and ill intended elected officials and their bureaucrats have clearly proven that **we must fight city hall**!!!

The lack of solid grounding and sincere leadership ..

coupled oftentimes with selfish plans and agendas ..

is literally, destroying this Country and its future!!!

We do have a lot of work to do; so let's get started. We have the tools. We are a capable society. There's no good reason to delay.

Let's get busy ..

Help me in my run for President .. with you.

<u>So What Are We Up Against</u>?

"We seek the complete destruction of the United States of America."

"Our goal is to destroy American capitalism and all it represents."

"The mission is to eradicate the American way of life."

"We will bury America and never fire a shot."

Digest those words. Close your eyes and focus in on someone, some group or organization, some country or countries .. proclaiming those things.

Proclaiming them because they truly, truly mean them!

Most Americans find this sort of talk absurd. "Impossible." "Simply ain't gonna happen." "No way – never happen here."

The routine and even expected response to these declarations would commonly be surprise and utter disbelief.

Many Americans will be troubled and deeply saddened to hear the words calling for the absolute end of America.

All .. will want to believe that it will never happen.

Truth is .. as much as we hate to admit it or believe .. **America, and all it represents, does have enemies!!!**

Enemies who want us dead and gone. Enemies that feel just as strongly about us being the "Great Satan" and the source of poison to the globe, as we feel that we are a source of goodness and justice.

We cannot continue to be in that place of complacency that says, "we'll always succeed because of who and what we are – the United States of America".

We have to be alert to the fact that we do have enemies. Capable enemies. Active enemies who are aggressively strategizing our downfall and implementing their game plans.

I'd like to draw your attention to some of the strategies uncovered by W. Cleon Skousen, a Chief Advisor to the FBI, Founder of the National Center for Constitutional Studies, and author of "The 5000 Year Leap".

In the 1940's, he spoke in detail about some progressive goals and outlined them in his book, "Naked Communism". These goals .. this strategy .. are parts of a plan to bring about the complete collapse and demise of America.

The "game plan" that they have developed and implemented as long ago as the 1940's is a thorough one and very do-able.

Not only do I want to alert you to this strategy, I want you to carefully read the following goals that I've listed; and then make a decision on whether that goal is being, or has been, accomplished here in America.

My guess is that you'll be very, very surprised at just how many of those goals that you may agree that have been accomplished.

Approach this important exercise with an open mind. Be thoughtful and honest with your decisions on their completion. Here are a few parts of the plan:

- Promote the U.N. as the only hope for mankind. If its charter is rewritten, demand that it be set up as one world government with its own independent armed forces.

- Do away with all loyalty oaths.

- Capture one or both of the political parties in the U.S.

- Use technical decisions of the courts to weaken basic American institutions by claiming their activities violate civil rights.

- Get control of the schools. Use them as transmission belts for socialism and current Socialist propaganda. Soften the curriculum. Get control of the teachers' associations. Put the party line in the textbooks.

- Gain control of all student newspapers.

- Use student riots to foment public protests against programs or organizations which are under Socialist attack.

- Infiltrate the press. Get control of book review assignments, editorial writing, and policy making positions.

- Gain control of key positions in radio, TV and motion pictures.

- Continue discrediting American culture by degrading all forms of artistic expression.

- Control art critics and directors of art museums. "Our plan is to promote ugliness, repulsive meaningless art."

- Eliminate all laws governing obscenity by calling them "censorship" and a violation of free speech and free press.

- Break down cultural standards of morality by promoting pornography and obscenity in books, magazines, motion pictures, radio and TV.

- Present homosexuality, degeneracy and promiscuity as "normal, natural, and healthy."

- Infiltrate the churches and replace revealed religion with "social" religion. Discredit the Bible and emphasize the need for intellectual maturity which does not need a "religious crutch."

- Eliminate prayer or any phase of religious expression in the schools on the ground that it violates the principle of "separation of church and state."

- Discredit the American Constitution by calling it inadequate, old-fashioned, out of step with modern needs, a hindrance to cooperation between nations on a world-wide basis.

- Discredit the American Founding Fathers. Present them as selfish aristocrats who had no concern for the "common man."

- Belittle all forms of American culture and discourage the teaching of American history on the grounds it was only a minor part of "the big picture" of social studies.

- Support any socialist movement to give centralized control over any part of the culture – education, social agencies, welfare programs, mental health clinics, etc.

- Discredit and eventually dismantle the FBI.

- Infiltrate and gain control of more unions.

- Infiltrate and gain control of big business.

- Transfer some of the powers of arrest from the police to social agencies. Treat all behavioral problems as psychiatric disorders which no one but a psychiatrist can understand or treat.

- Discredit the family as an institution. Encourage promiscuity and easy divorce.

- Emphasize the need to raise children away from the negative influence of parents. Attribute prejudices, mental blocks and retarding of children to suppressive influence of parents.

- Create the impression that violence and insurrection are legitimate aspects of the American tradition: that students and special-interest groups should rise up and use "united force" to solve economic, political or social problems.

Quite a list, 'ay.

You also need to know this is only about 2/3rds of that list.

Isn't it a bit amazing, a bit scary even, that we can review a list of this nature and know that a huge percentage of the goals to bring about the destruction of America from within have been enacted and in the works for seventy plus years?

More scary .. they are being accomplished!!!

This is not something to take lightly. It is not something to breeze past and write off as some vast conspiracy theory.

Read the list!!!

Go back over it and genuinely reflect upon those bullet points that resonate with your observations and experiences. This is serious, serious business.

And just as serious is .. **what are we going to do about it?**

Whenever I'm able to share this exercise in a group setting, I always take a poll of the groups responses and find that most folks will generally agree that a minimum of 33 of the 45 goals have been accomplished, or, are definitely underway in a very significant manner here in this country.

Breathtaking!

An enemy of this country has outlined a game plan for the collapse and destruction of America; and they have accomplished, at minimum, 33 of their 45 goals.

May as well say more than 2/3rds of their plans have succeeded.

And sadly, it has been said that, **"Many of the goals have been achieved right under the nose of sleepy and apathetic Americans."**

None of us want to believe this is happening; but I'm going to encourage you to go back over your list and your findings. How many goals do you see being accomplished?

It could be to our continued and certain peril to overlook the very active aggression(s) being purposefully thrust upon our nation.

Review your findings. Share this activity with your friends, families, and acquaintances. Take that honest look at where we're at individually and as a nation. Talk about it with those you know and trust.

Let it be a task to help start some honest soul searching. Let it be a task to begin a string of commitments to actively help start to turn some things around in this Country.

Become part of the solution .. instead of part of the problem.

It really does appear that the "American frog" is being boiled.

You know the story.

A frog dropped into a pot of boiling water will do anything possible to escape; but if you put him in when the pot is full of cool water and gradually turn up the heat .. the frog will acclimate to the water and eventually boil and die.

How hot is the water? Have we begun to boil?

I'm running for President to help turn the heat off.

Will you join me?

So How Do We Turn the Heat Down?

The first step in resolving most problems is to recognize that they are present and are a "problem".

Amongst all the things that are happening in the world today .. amongst all the anti-American rhetoric and animosity towards the U.S. .. and amongst all the real enemies we face .. the things that we just reviewed - those 45 bullet points - are a very toxic acid eating away at the foundations of America.

They are, indeed, part of the life blood and heart beat of our nation's enemy within.

In addition to the destructiveness of the 45 "progressive" goals that have been eating away at the American fiber for more than a half of a century, there is the added danger of our own apathy and foolhardiness that needs to be looked at.

Now as I say that, I need to be very clear about some absolute truths that I hold about most Americans. They include:

- I believe many – to most - Americans are very kind, very gracious, very helpful, and very honest people with admirable and sincere intentions, morals, and ethics.

- I believe that many – to most - Americans truly love their Country and respect its Founding and heritage.

- I believe that many – to most – Americans believe in, and try to foster, an orderly and civil society guided by the rule of law.

- I believe that many – to most – Americans would be honored to serve their Country and if needed, die for it.

- I believe that many – to most – Americans truly embrace the spirit in the words of our 35th President, the late John F. Kennedy, who said, "Ask not what your Country can do for you; but what <u>you</u> can do for your Country."

- And I believe, more and more, with each passing day, that many – to most – Americans are becoming increasingly fed up with the very, very dangerous cloud of deception and destruction that is enshrouding our nation and is being caused by a multitude of our leaders and bureaucrats - as seriously derelict and misguided as they are.

- I also believe that we are at the critical boiling point (if not a bit beyond)!!!

We must acknowledge that and take immediate steps to change our course .. to turn the flame off!!!

Notice that while listing my beliefs about Americans, I said "many – to most". I did that for a very specific reason.

Because it's true!!!

I fully well believe that most Americans fall on the good side of those things I mentioned. Good and gracious people who love and honor their Country and all it represents. People who are grateful for their, and their Country's blessings; and do hope to safeguard and preserve them for their posterity and even the world.

But I also believe, and know, there are unfortunately far too many Americans that could care less about any of those things and that are absolutely more concerned about what they can get .. how they can play the system .. what's in it for them .. now, tomorrow, and for as long as they want and can take.

Give nothing .. take as much as can be had .. and <u>demand</u> more!!!

Not long ago, I viewed a video from a Town Hall meeting hosted by none other than the Congresswoman Maxine Waters. One of her supporters brought crystal clear vision to her (and most all of the others in attendance) stance and position when she vigorously and demonstratively proclaimed that she "wanted to know what her country was going to do for her <u>right now</u>!!!"

She, Ms. Waters, and their fellow Town Hall attendees were fairly certain that the current administration simply was not doing anywhere near enough for the "African-American" population here in America.

What a huge departure from President Kennedy's words of, "Ask not what your Country can do for you .." to the arrogant and self-serving demands of an overfed leach on the Country's goodness.

"What is my country going to do for me .. <u>now</u>!!!"

Where, oh where, did this twisted, self-serving, and self-centered attitude come from?

Why, oh why, is it allowed to permeate its tenants throughout our society and culture and become an expected part of the norm?

Where will this twisted sort of thinking, living, and expecting .. demanding even .. lead us?

I'd propose to nowhere good!

It hasn't thus far .. and that simply won't change!

It can get worse .. and it may .. but it won't get better without some serious and sincere effort by many!

Fortunately, most Americans don't fall into this self-centered and greedy spot. Most Americans definitely want to provide for their families and themselves; as well as to help others that may not be as fortunate.

But there is a very large, and growing, body of folks that concretely feel that they are owed something by just about everybody. They are the constant victims .. the forever downtrodden .. the folks that are just always getting the unfair side of the coin .. and consequently, are not getting all they deserve – through no fault of their own, of course.

They're pretty well convinced that there is just nothing they can ever do to get ahead; and that everyone, and everything, is against them and they will never do well or have as much as the next guy.

They are the permanent losers in life's lottery.

Poor me .. poor me .. and poor me.

Always and forever, poor me. And because of that, you owe me.

Amazing!!!

We happen to live in the absolute breadbasket of the world .. the hub of the greatest opportunity anywhere on the globe .. the freest land and center of more liberty to be enjoyed than anywhere .. and by some cosmic happenstance, we have huge portions of the population that are completely incapable and incompetent to the degree of being unable to care and provide for themselves.

Should I add, may I add, "even if they wanted to?"

Again .. amazing!!!

So .. we have the destructiveness of the 45 "progressive" goals that are eating away at the American fiber and have been for more than half of a century. Then we add a very large and eager army of the self acclaimed "downtrodden" to the mix that are past ready to "even the score"; throw in a hefty handful of "special interests" die-hards .. and we have an extremely toxic stew brewing. An explosive and corrosive stew. A mixture that can deeply scar, if not destroy, America.

Dangerous ingredients. An astronomically detrimental recipe. And especially poisonous when brewed and spiced by our very own leaders. A brew that will be most thorough and destructive when spoon fed to us by the folks we have entrusted to be our "leaders" .. our "guardians'' .. our "public servants".

We begin to turn the heat down when we accept that there are accomplished enemies that have been chipping away at our way of life for a very long time, that there's a pretty large crowd of folks who feel a need to get even with the metaphorical "US" (us), and that a very large collection of our leaders are aiding and abetting these "enemies" (knowingly, or not).

We begin to turn the heat down when we engage in the corrective measures that will be required to get our Country .. the grandest and greatest example of self-governance, freedom, and liberty ever known to mankind .. back on solid footing and prudent practices.

We begin to turn the heat down when we get involved with the "fix"!!!

That is why I'm running for President .. and hoping you'll join me!!!

So Much Hardship. So much Challenge.

Where, and how, do we begin?

Most all Americans are very aware of the problems. Many have healthy assortments of solutions. But .. there's always going to be differing positions on just about everything.

So .. we begin an immediate and massive campaign of renewing the concept and practice of "Public Service – Public Servants" and a return to the true and real duties of the Federal Government as outlined .. as assigned to it .. by "We the People" in our Constitution.

America is a fabulous country. We were founded under the inspiration of certain principles, beliefs, and truths.

Our Founders .. our Country's Framers .. went to great lengths to become very familiar with many, to all, forms of government. They thoroughly discussed and debated their plans for this government. They vehemently argued their positions and fought hard to put the things in place that would guide and sustain this country indefinitely.

They built a nation and formed a government that was unique to the world in many ways. They brought to the forefront the notion of people self-governing themselves; not being ruled by class or dictate, not by conquerors or tyrants, but by themselves – guided by a constitution and a commitment to the rule of law versus the rule of men.

They called upon, and relied upon, Divine Providence to protect them, to guide them, and to aid them in bringing about this great nation – a nation that would be the most significant example to mankind of self-governance, liberty, and freedom ever!

Our Founders engaged in the first "Nation Building" project ever!

And what a terrific job they did. America has been richly blessed and has been able to be a haven of the absolute best the world has to offer mankind for a long, long time.

Being mindful of this, our immediate pursuit will be a focused and specific chain of efforts to return this Country to the very things that helped create our extremely successful and rewarding existence.

We will return to the wisdom and guidance of the Constitution!!!

We will encourage a renewed and refreshed embracement of the Declaration of Independence!!!

The answers to our problems and difficulties lie within the remedies that are contained in the structure of those documents. We, as a nation, as a people, have wandered far from the spirit directed by those documents; so a renewed embracement of them is long overdue and an extremely healthy effort.

Yes .. there will be many that will scoff and attack this notion as foolish! There will be many who claim that those documents are old, irrelevant, antique, and simply worthless at this point of our history!

(Remember the list of 45 goals?)

I would argue .. as President .. and with you by my side .. that those documents will absolutely guide us out of our troubles and secure a positive and rewarding future for us now and for our posterity. Without question .. without doubt. Our task .. our combined task as a nation .. will be to engage in an honest and concentrated effort to get that job done.

No half measures. No fudging. Patience will be required.

We will all have to sacrifice some.

But .. we can return this nation to its greatness.

And that goal of returning to our nation's greatness should propel us to another long overdue project of significant importance. Revisiting and relearning our nation's true history from start to finish .. top to bottom.

How did those concepts our Founders sought to integrate into our national fiber .. our national existence .. come to be?

What are the concepts .. the values .. the principles our Founders viewed as so important to the success of our great nation?

Big question .. have you read the Declaration of Independence? Be honest. When was the last time you read it? How intensely did you study and discuss it? What does it mean to you today?

Do you know that the things our Founders cited in our Declaration to the King of England as objectionable pale in comparison to much of the injustices our government asserts upon us today?

Another big question .. have you read the Constitution for the United States? Be honest. When was the last time you read that, if ever? How intensely did you study and discuss it? What does that document mean to you today?

If you've read it, do you see the gross disregard to it perpetrated by the supposed combined leadership of today and recent times past?

There can be no confusion .. the Constitution of this Country is being dramatically ignored and abused severely by those sworn to defend and uphold it; and that has been occurring for a long, long time now.

If the abuses to the Constitution are allowed to continue, it is <u>certain</u> that this experiment in self-governance <u>will fail</u>!!!

Our freedoms and liberties will continue to dissolve!!!

The abuses are taking place through lack of knowledge and concern, or, because of more sinister reasons. No reason is acceptable and the abuses must stop immediately.

Any person with reasonable intelligence and concern for this great nation can read the Constitution; and armed with that knowledge can see the disregard and abuse that's in place.

So, yes .. I'll be running for President .. ideally with you.

And we will launch a national initiative to return our Country to Constitutional Governance ..   Day #1.

Let's run.

Sounds Like Trouble Already

Will we be well received with this Constitutional appeal?

Likely not.

Likely not by many; but I suspicion our idea of returning to Constitutional Governance will be well received and welcomed by most.

At the start of the 112th Congress in 2011, Congressional leadership proposed opening its session with the reading of the Constitution.

My God!!!

The yelping and whining that went on over that request was shameful. The left .. the "progressives" .. thought it was being done for theatrics. They thought it was a meaningless waste of time. They felt that it was a game being orchestrated by the right.

Imagine ... reading the instruction manual before beginning the activity.

Woe are we! How very 'stone age'!?!?

How telling were the objections to the reading of the Constitution at the opening of the session! How revealing a picture of those who were in such contempt of the idea!

Their combined objections really speaks volumes and tells us a lot about those objecting. Those folks assembled in that body take an oath that includes a promise "to uphold and defend the Constitution of the United States".

God forbid that they know what is in it!?!?

What can be the sincerity and depth of their oaths based upon their lack of knowledge concerning the Constitution?

Was taking the oath sincere or simply a photo op?

We had a Speaker of the House in Nancy Pelosi who answered a reporter's question on the constitutionality of the national health care legislation with, "That can't be a serious question!" "That's not a serious question!"

Because her response caused such a stir in mature circles, her office had to double down on her very inept and insane response by saying "the Speaker stands with her response – that was not a serious question".

Absolutely breathtaking that we can have a Speaker of the House of Representatives of the United States Congress who feels as though a question from a citizen about the Constitutionality of a piece of legislation can't be a serious question – and mean it!

Of course, this came from the same misguided Speaker who let us know that, "we have to pass the Bill to know what's in it."

Imagine doing business with someone who instructs you to sign the contract so you can then know what's in it.

You wouldn't do business with them!

The Madame Speaker (and her sidekicks) should be ashamed at the utter lunacy in such a posture – "pass the Bill so we can know what's in it.".

<u>Our Founders were likely spinning in their graves over that!!!</u>

Then, of course, we can illustrate the outrageous opposition to the Constitution by fast forwarding to the banner article in "Time" magazine on – believe it or not – the 4th of July, 2011, that poses the theory that the Constitution really doesn't matter anymore and pictures it going through a shredder.

<u>Stunning</u> .. <u>Breathtaking</u>

An article that completely trashes our Constitution on none other than the day we celebrate our Country's independence and the beginning of the journey into the world's very first experience in self-governance .

Especially breathtaking and stunning because of the day of public release of the article – the 4th of July – Independence Day; but also because of the purposeful misinformation and typical venom that's included in the "progressive's" pursuits to undermine America's greatness.

So, yes .. there will be opposition to the idea of returning to the Constitution as the guide for managing our Country's affairs. The usual host of nay sayers will be abundant; but we must be resolute. Our answers **are** in our Founding Documents and we must reinstitute their guiding light.

The opposition will be very vocal. Their tactics to detract from our mission will be many and creative. You can bet there will be huge push back against a return to the restraints of the Constitution.

The thrust against a return to the Constitution will be driven out of the lust to retain power and influence.

It will be driven by the desire for money. Those opposing a return to the Constitution likely see themselves being a bit neutered and likely to lose ground financially.

The loudest and most immediate disdain for the idea will be from those whose agendas are not at all truthful about "what's good for the Country."; and they will be loud. Boisterous even. Hopefully, peaceful.

We need to be prepared for any sort of reaction. We know, or certainly need to know, that those who oppose the restraints of the Constitution are the ones who are likely guilty of the most, the most frequent, and the largest improprieties against it. They will not easily surrender their "gravy train existence" supported by way of a runaway government operating outside the boundaries of our Constitution.

I'm anxious to bring this concept of Constitutional Governance to the forefront of the national discussion. It will be the beginning of the extraction from our hardships and dilemmas; and the push our Country needs to move forward in a productive manner.

It's the biggest reason that "I'll be running for President".

Run with me .. I need you!

We the People
establish this CONSTITUTION for the United States of America.

But Aren't We Being Governed by the Constitution?

Not really. We haven't been for some time now.

"Well, goodness .. the politicians talk about it all the time."

There's a wonderful scene in the movie, "The Wizard of Oz".

Remember when Dorothy meets the scarecrow? They talk for a while and the scarecrow tells Dorothy he'd like to go to Oz with her and see if the Wizard could help him out with a brain.

Right?

Well .. our dear Dorothy says to the scarecrow, "You must have a brain."

To which the scarecrow replies, "Why do you say that, Dorothy?"

"Because you're talking," she says. "You <u>must</u> have a brain."

To which the scarecrow replies, "Oh, Dorothy. There are a lot of people who do a lot of talking that don't have any brains."

What a great scene! What a huge statement!

"There are a lot of people who do a lot of talking that don't have any brains."

39

I certainly am not going to say that there are a lot of people who "don't have brains"; but I would go so far as to say that quite oftentimes folks will certainly speak to issues way beyond their knowledge level .. for whatever reason.

I also know that oftentimes people will repeat things .. report things .. simply because that's what they were told or taught. Altogether too often, folks simply will not research things with any intensity if what they're being told seems reasonable or possible to them.

If I made the comment that I had a cute little "widget" that dates back to the late 1700's and does basic math, folks might think that "widget" kind of novel .. kind of cute; but certainly outdated for today's purposes.

So when that Constitution from the late 1700's is said to be old and outdated .. it's easy for folks to grasp that thought and agree with it. It might even be somewhat normal to just file that tidbit of information in the "don't need to know" category or even the "irrelevant" bin of our minds.

Add to that some passion fueled by purposeful misinformation or specific agendas that are being taught (remember the goals of discounting our heritage and discrediting our Founders) and we can have a set of very misleading and damaging outcomes.

Probably, the best and most classic example of Constitutional misinformation is this whole notion of separation of church and state that supposedly exists in the Constitution. I have read and studied the Constitution in much more detail and frequency than most folks, and I have never seen that proposed separation presented in the document.

However, the constant drumbeat of "progressive" teaching and thought demands an absolute belief that this alleged separation of church and state exists and is in the Constitution.

It really, really is not in the Constitution!!!

There's no one that can point to the text in the Constitution that says there shall be a separation of church and state. As a matter of fact, if a person really goes in search of an honest answer to that question, they would have to go no further than taking a walk around our nation's Capitol buildings. You will see purposeful and visible symbolism recognizing Divinity all over the place - even inside the buildings.

Read the writings of the Founders themselves and you will see almost constant reference to the Divine.

Check out George Washington's "Thanksgiving Day Proclamation" and try to convince anyone that's read that, that George .. our very first President .. our first Commander-in-Chief .. the fellow generally recognized as the Father of our Country .. felt a need for this imagined "separation".

On the contrary, in Washington's proclamation he starts by saying, **".. it is the duty of all nations to acknowledge the providence of Almighty God, to obey His will, to be grateful for His benefits, and humbly implore His protection and favour .."**

Question .. **If the Founders .. the Framers .. of our Country intended for this "separation of church and state" ... why is there such a huge presence of the Divine in the seat of our national government and in so, so many of the Founders writings?**

A common sense response to that honest exploration really says that this supposed separation is a huge figment of someone's imagination or agenda – for whatever reasons.

There is a large body of thought that says there's a very focused effort to remove God from our national existence. I certainly would agree that there is a very purposeful effort to remove God from our national existence.

Take a look back at the ugly list of goals to destroy America. You bet there's a focus on removing God from the national landscape.

Look how long the drum has been beaten about the separation of church and state. It's been beaten long enough and hard enough that most folks believe it exists.

The truth is that it simply does not!

Not long ago, I was asked to be interviewed by a local news outlet. They wanted to ask me some questions concerning conservatism and my thoughts on the TEA Party. I explained to the individual that I'd be happy to do that; but would expect to be quoted in entirety or be given the opportunity to review what would be put in print <u>before</u> it was put in print.

Of course, this newsman wasn't comfortable with those conditions and thought my terms would really slow the process uncomfortably so. As a result, I turned down the interview. The fellow that was pursuing the chat didn't seem too happy with leaving empty handed; so he began to try and quiz me about the "state of the union" with some random and benign kinds of questions.

I let him know again that if he was looking to gather some printable stuff .. the same rules applied that I'd just mentioned. A little bit out of frustration, I think, he finally blurted out, "So what do you think is the biggest problem here in this country?".

I let him know that I'd be happy to answer that and did answer him by saying that I think the biggest problems in this Country stem from our straying so far from, and so routinely ignoring, our Country's Founding Documents – especially the Constitution. I asserted to him that the answers to most of our difficulties - on at least a federal level - are in the sincere application of that document – especially Article 1, Section 8.

I could tell that he had absolutely no idea what I was talking about so I asked him, "Have you ever read the Constitution?"

Now, I've never met this man. My guess is that he's probably in his late 40's or early 50's. He seemed of average intelligence; but it was clear that he had an agenda and that was that conservatives and conservatism, as well as those TEA Party folks, are a little bit out there on the fringe. After all, isn't that the drum beat? Isn't that the hoped for agenda? .. the desired propaganda?

To his credit, he did answer my question to him honestly. His response to the question of his reading the Constitution was, "No. I haven't."

And isn't it amazing how often the honest answer to that question – "Have you read the Constitution?" – is most usually, "No. I haven't."

And at the same time, isn't that tragically sad?

I suggested to my news friend that he read the Constitution and call me back. I encouraged him by letting him know that once he read it, we could have a much more intelligent and productive discussion.

He never called back and I doubt he read it.

Amazing that we'll read the intellectually dishonest propaganda that "Time" magazine spews. We'll listen to the purposeful misinformation of members of academia, the media and politicians who pontificate their slanted versions of all sorts, and we'll succumb to the loudest chatter around the water cooler; but rarely do we take the time to investigate on our own and actually read the document(s).

Because I'll be running for President .. hopefully with you .. part of our overall efforts will be to encourage every American to read the Constitution for the United States and become very familiar with it.

It takes about 45 minutes to an hour to read and will certainly help folks determine if their government is functioning as designed.

Truth be known, the federal government has long ago gone very destructively beyond the limits placed upon it by our Constitution. As a result, our Country is being driven to absolute insolvency, utter chaos and collapse.

Please, please, please .. do a very constructive American thing to do.

.. Read the Constitution ..

Then join me in this run for President.

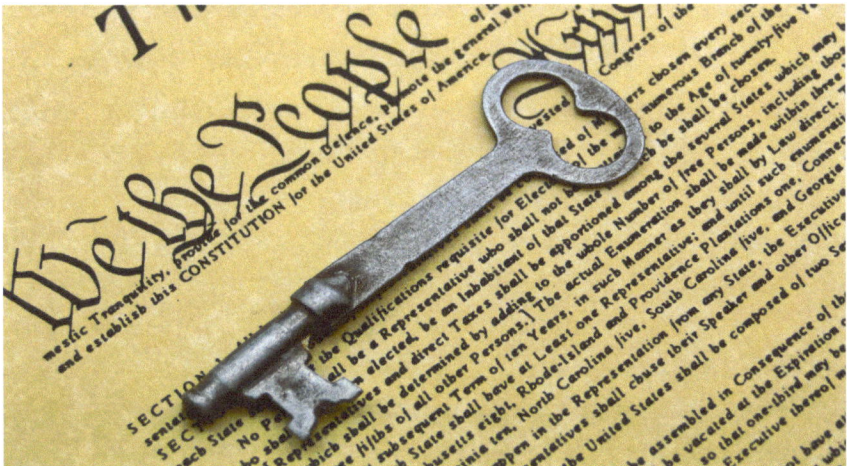

You Seem to be Really Convinced About This Constitution Thing!!!

I am very, very convinced that the honest and sincere application of our Constitution .. the Constitution for the United States .. will restore us to a much healthier position here at home and will also help to reflect a much more productive vision of America, and Americans, to the world.

Yes .. I am absolutely convinced of that!!!

Several years ago, I was in discussion with a fellow who had studied the Constitution in pretty significant detail. His very adamant pet peeve surrounding the document was the misguided belief of the "separation of church and state"; but he had also studied some of the other ramifications to our nation that are being created as a result of the unconstitutional behaviors undertaken by the federal government that happen on a regular basis. Through his studies, he had determined that roughly 70% of the activities our federal government involves itself in are not authorized by our Constitution.

At a glance, and being reasonably knowledgeable about the Constitution as well, I'm certainly not going to dispute his claim(s). I'm comfortable with his studied determination that suggests that, at minimum, 70% of the federal government's activities and involvements are unconstitutional.

So .. carry that conversation .. that equation .. into a monetary proposal. Loosely said, could it be argued then that 70% of the dollars the federal government expends are done so unconstitutionally and thereby, in an unauthorized manner? They simply don't have the Constitutional authority to spend the money.

If ... we held the federal government's feet to the fire and restrained it by the limits spelled out in our Constitution ... **imagine** ... instead of them coming to us and demanding more and more dollars for them to seize and squander .. to plunge our debt to others over the $16 trillion dollar mark and counting .. **We, the People .. tell them how many dollars they will get to fulfill their assigned duties!**

"We, the people," .. can put a cost figure to the duties that the federal government is constitutionally charged to do. History and the benefit of experience will help us determine those amounts. Their duties are listed in Article 1, Section 8 of the Constitution. Those are the things that they are supposed to involve themselves with – they are the "Enumerated Powers" granted to the federal government.

Knowledgeable of the federal governments duties and using that formula, 'We, the people," are in a position that we can tell them what they get to spend versus them telling us what they intend to spend. If they are not good stewards of our dollars and don't get their jobs done, they need to lose their positions as quickly as possible – through impeachment or by soonest vote.

No longer will our federal leadership get to throw our money around with foolhardy abandon!

No longer will our federal leadership get to secure their positions by purchasing votes with taxpayer dollars and under the guise of "doing good for the Country"!

No longer do they get to cement their positions by taking care of their buddies and favored special interest groups!

We, the people, will be telling them what they get to spend!!!

<u>The Constitution will tell them on what they'll spend!!!</u>

And yes .. our administration .. yours and mine .. will usher this restorative change into the nation's capitol and welcome it!!!

You need to know that there's really nothing much new to this theory of the federal government spending money that they are not constitutionally authorized to. Astute minds that are paying attention to the goings on of D.C. have approached this issue in a variety of ways over the years.

John Shattug, a former Congressman from Arizona, has introduced the "Enumerated Powers Act" in every session of Congress since 1996. That Act says pretty simply that Congress shall cite their constitutional authority for every piece of legislation they handle <u>before</u> they attempt to make it law.

Said another way, if they cannot find the Constitutional authority for a proposed bill, they need to "can it". No authority – no law made – no money spent.

In contrast, look at the billions of dollars that have already been spent on the completely unconstitutional ObamaCare legislation.

Nowhere in our Constitution is the federal government empowered to be in the business of healthcare; but look at the money that's been exhausted.

Tragic .. shameful .. and unlawful.

Sounds like a very good idea this "Enumerated Powers Act". Sounds like it would go a long way to control and manage federal spending.

That could be why the "Enumerated Powers Act" has never made its way out of initial committees.

Its passage (and if adhered to and enforced) would effectively neuter those who are misusing their "power" and eliminate huge loop holes that graft and corruption fall through.

Just prior to the elections in November 2010, the Republicans promised in their "Pledge to America" that they would also cite Constitutional authority for every bill they handled; and that they would strictly adhere to the Constitution.

Apparently that pledge was only for before the elections. Their promise, too, unfortunately, has not been fulfilled.

As I'll be running for President .. with you .. we will get this overdue and necessary piece of America's restoration done!!!

Seems Like a Massive Undertaking

Where will we begin?

How will we manage to get this done?

You're right.

It is a very massive undertaking; but indeed an undertaking that needs to be embarked upon. To continue along the paths we've been on will be to enable and patronize the continued destruction of the United States of America and all it represents.

I .. we .. will not be any part of the destruction of America!!!

Immediately .. Day 1, as the politicks say .. we'll begin implementing our agenda. Doing the things we'll need to do to show folks that ..

- Our purpose is to be of sound and meaningful **service** to America and its citizens. It is not to govern by dictate because "I (we) won!"; but to serve the Country while sincerely and honestly upholding and defending the Constitution.

- The idea and living spirit of "public servant" and "public service" will be re-introduced into the entire arena of the public sphere.

  Our very first president, George Washington, always felt that it was the honor of his life to again serve his Country and be its first President. Never, would have Washington, or any other of the

Founders, uttered into a debate or discussion with an American citizen that, "I won. Get over it."

We will commit to doing all we can to foster the idea and spirit of "public service" at all levels of governance.

- Our mission is to return the activities of the federal government to those activities authorized to it by the Constitution. The first step of that process will be to carefully review and define those duties as outlined in Article 1, Section 8 of the Constitution; and then help to implement procedures to get in compliance with the Constitution and Article 1, Section 8.

This work will be an amazing undertaking. We will be returning huge portions of federal influence and activity back to where it belongs - in the States and the people.

We will need help, we will need patience and understanding, and we will need the American public's involvement. Our work will always be completely transparent and we will be certain to do our best to keep America involved and informed.

This return to Constitutional compliance, however, will be our primary mission and focus.

Again, on that famous Day 1, we will <u>begin</u> to conduct very active workshops with the Governors of all 50 States (the 44th President speaks of 57 States; however, I'm only aware of the 50 that are each signified by a brilliant white star on our nation's flag).

We'll begin to gather their thoughts and ideas surrounding this national shift back to consistency with the Constitution and Article 1, Section 8. After all, the States will be taking on duties and tasks that belonged in their jurisdictions in the first place; and we will need an assortment of cooperative efforts with a battery of resources from within the States to help accommodate these shifts.

We'll also be asking Congress to begin their honest and careful review and determinations concerning the federal government and its agencies being in complete compliance with Article 1, Section 8 of the Constitution.

This, of course, is where we'll hear the gang heralding the host of privileges and unbridled authority they have (which usually equates to spending money and buying votes) because of the Commerce Clause, the General Welfare Clause, the Necessary and Proper Clause, and the newly popular, Good and Plenty Clause.

You know .. those magical "Clauses" they use to justify doing just about anything they want or think that will help get them re-elected.

This is where one can tell who has read the Constitution and who hasn't. This is where one can tell if the reader's comprehension level is ninth grade or above. This is where you'll see the biggest efforts to guard the scam that's been going on and keep it going.

Those "Clauses" .. that particular language .. does appear in the Constitution (except, of course, the Good and Plenty Clause which falls into the same fuzzy area of thought that another current Congressman had when he worried that the island of Guam would tip over if we stationed a few more Marines on it); but it appears as part of a larger statement. They do not appear as individual and unique statements or grants of authority – "clauses".

These imagined "clauses" have been being abused and misused for decades. They have enabled our "leaders" to overreach their authority repeatedly. By design and original intent, our Constitution was to restrain the government from doing whatever it feels it wants to do .. <u>under any clause</u> – real or imagined!

But .. lawyer-ese, political wordsmithing, and an apathetic response from "We the People" has enabled our leaders (of all political stripes) to run amuck with these supposed authorities and create extremely dangerous and costly violations of our Constitution – accumulatively towards our complete insolvency and destruction.

Our Founders .. our Framers .. provided a handful of straightforward and common sense warnings to these encroachments upon our Constitution and the repetitively costly attacks.

Let's see what some of them had to say ...

"The powers delegated by the proposed Constitution to the Federal Government, are **FEW AND DEFINED**. Those which are to remain in the State Governments are **NUMEROUS AND INDEFINITE**. The former will be exercised principally on external objects, as war, peace, negotiation, and foreign commerce; with which last the power of taxation will for the most part be connected.

The powers reserved to the several States will extend to all the objects, which, in the ordinary course of affairs, concern the lives, liberties and properties of the people; and the internal order, improvement, and prosperity of the State." - James Madison, Federalist No. 45, 1788 (emphasis added)

In condensed speech .. federal government small and defined; State government .. what do you and your citizens want to do?

James Madison again from a speech in 1788 .. "The powers of the federal government are <u>enumerated</u>; it can only operate in certain cases; it has legislative powers on defined and limited objects, <u>beyond which it cannot extend its jurisdiction</u>."

In short .. the duties of the federal government are listed – they have no grant of authority to go beyond those listed duties.

In 1792, during the First Congressional floor debate, James Madison said, "If Congress can employ money indefinitely to the GENERAL WELFARE, and are the sole and supreme judges of the GENERAL WELFARE, they may take the care of religion into their own hands; they may appoint teachers in every State, county, and parish and pay them out of the public treasury; they may take into their own hands the education of children, establishing in like manner schools throughout the Union; they may assume the provision of the poor, they may undertake the regulation of all roads other than post-roads; in short, <u>EVERYTHING</u>, from the highest object of State legislation down to the most minute object of police, would be thrown under the power of Congress ... were the powers of Congress to be established in the latitude contended for, IT WOULD SUBVERT THE VERY FOUNDATIONS, AND TRANSMUTE THE VERY NATURE OF THE LIMITED GOVERNMENT ESTABLISHED BY THE PEOPLE OF AMERICA."

Translates to .. Keep the Federal Government small and limited! Don't let it get out of line and destroy what we're all about!

And isn't it very amazing that the Federal authorities are attempting to do each and every item our Founders warned us against!

The always popular Thomas Jefferson gave us terrific direction through his next two comments concerning "General Welfare" by saying in 1791, "It would reduce the whole instrument [the Constitution] to a single phrase, that of instituting a Congress with power to do whatever would be for the good of the United States; and as they would be the sole judges of the good or evil, it would also be a power to do whatever evil they please. CERTAINLY NO SUCH UNIVERSAL POWER WAS MEANT TO BE GIVEN TO THEM. IT [the Constitution] WAS INTENDED TO LACE THEM UP STRAIGHTLY WITHIN THE ENUMERATED POWERS and those without which, as means, these powers could not be carried into effect."

He revisited his thoughts on the subject again in 1817 by saying, "Congress has not unlimited powers to provide for the general welfare, but only those specifically enumerated."

In other words, reflective of the two quotations .. the federal government really has no power to act at their will, justifying their actions by claiming, "for the general welfare". In all that they do, they <u>must</u> stay within the confines of what the Constitution authorizes them to do within the parameters of the enumerated powers in Article 1, Section 8.

Well, well, well.

So what about the "Necessary and Proper" clause? Doesn't that give them carte blanche authority to do whatever is "necessary"?

The folks that want to continue to abuse our nation and steal our wealth may hang onto that flimsy reed; but again, here's a terrific example of why it's important to read and know the document.

The final paragraph of Article 1, Section 8 – you know, the Section that talks about what the federal government is empowered to do - says, "To make all Laws which shall be **<u>necessary and proper</u> FOR CARRYING INTO EXECUTION THE FOREGOING POWERS, and all other Powers <u>VESTED BY THIS CONSTITUTION</u> ...**".

So once we read the document, we learn that the imaginary powers and latitudes these folks have been wielding while they regulate the air right out of us and empty our Treasury for generations are without any truthful or prudent merit.

A bunch of lawyers and judges playing lawyer-ese and word games while they prey on the citizen's goodwill and lack of information and understanding.

So you bet .. we'll be engaging a lot of folks along with those Governors as we re-examine our Constitution and move back towards an honest and sincere return to it.

And as we encounter questions or confusion, we will seek answers by utilizing the thoughtful and very expert guidance of Mr. Thomas Jefferson that he offered by saying, "On every question of construction, let us carry ourselves back to the time when the Constitution was adopted, recollect the spirit manifested in the debates, and **INSTEAD OF TRYING WHAT MEANING MAY BE SQUEEZED OUT OF THE TEXT, OR INVENTED AGAINST IT,** conform to the probable one in which it was passed."

Most of us will recall the words, **"Original Intent"**. We can answer our Constitutional questions and concerns most effectively by remembering what the **Original Intent** of our Founders most likely was; recalling that one of the very cornerstones of all their efforts was to avoid a large and encompassing central government, and instead making sure that the federal influence was kept small and very limited to specific things.

Our Founders were very aware of the things to avoid and why!

Isn't it amazing how the violations of our Constitution have included most all of those things our Founders knew we had to avoid having happen; and that those continued violations are leading the Country into absolute chaos and complete collapse.

They warned us to avoid large and centralized government!

They told us not to allow them to put us in debt for generations!

They cautioned us to be "forever diligent".

It's past time to return to the wisdom of our Founders and the guidance they offered us in their many, many writings. The answers to our combined dilemmas are embodied in the Declaration of Independence, the Constitution, the Federalist and Anti-Federalist Papers, and in the honest representation of our Founders personal writings, experiences, and examples.

We need to tap into those treasure chests of wisdom!

And we will as we rebuild our Country through its return to Constitutional Governance.

Instead of photo op's and play office summits to give the air of doing something important, we will have meaningful and focused strategy sessions to accomplish our goals of returning the form of government that was designed for us to "We, the People, …".

What an invigorating mission for a President …

… <u>and</u> his running mate.

You still with me?

I'm Still With Ya'!

"We'll really be changing the "look" and the "feel" of the Country, won't we be?"

"Will people acclimate to the changes?"

We have reached a point in our Country's history where the largest part of our federal government's total expenditures go to entitlements, welfare, social programs, and other "give away" schemes. Roughly one out of five families in America receives some sort of government subsidy.

Nowhere in our Constitution will we see that a function or duty of the government is to be a charity or philanthropic entity. Matter of fact, our Founders warned against that. They knew the problems that would arise when government could use "gifts" for the people to garner their support. They knew how that concept would grow to disastrous proportions and cause dramatic misuses and abuses.

James Madison, the Father of our Constitution, wisely and accurately said in 1796, "I cannot undertake to lay my finger on that article of the Constitution which granted a right to Congress of expending, on objects of benevolence, the money of their constituents."

He was also to point out that, "With respect to the two words 'general welfare', I have always regarded them as qualified by the detail of powers connected with them. To take them in a literal and unlimited sense would be a metamorphosis of the Constitution into a character which there is a host of proofs was not contemplated by its creators."

And that .. is exactly what has been happening!!!

Our national leaders – and I use that term loosely - have gone well beyond their constitutionally prescribed duties; and are more interested in passing out the "chickens for every pot" so they can entrench their spot at the trough of the Treasury and retain a seat of unbridled power and influence in the swamplands of DC.

As we reintroduce the Constitution as the Supreme Law of the Land and the guide book for business on a federal level here in this Country, we will be changing the current "look and feel" of the government; but people will need to be mindful that we'll be changing it back to its original design. A design that works and one that will restore us to less chaos, confusion, and expense.

It did just that once already as we initially embarked on the journey of self-governance and Constitutional adherence.

Unconstitutional departments and agencies will be phased out and ultimately eliminated. Yes .. one of the money pits, the Department of Education, will be amongst the first. The United States currently spends more on education per pupil than any country in the world and has much worse outcomes.

In some recent interviews, some high school grads headed off for college thought that "bin Laden was the vice-president" and that there were as many as fifty three plus States in America.

(They may have been slightly misled by our first multi-racial president who calculated us having 57 some States.)

There is no legitimate reason for the Department of Education to continue to extort money for its bureaucracy that can be retained by the people and spent on more local levels for quality education. Parents, neighbors, and friends are far more capable of determining what their children should learn than the impersonal and selfish bureaucrats who are mainly interested in hanging onto their fat jobs, collecting their graft, and furthering their sick agendas.

Wasteful and unconstitutional federal programs and spending will be phased out and ultimately eliminated. Foreign aid will need to be scrutinized and paired back substantially, if not in most cases, eliminated. Our involvement in the United Nations needs complete review and overhaul; and those nations that care to participate in that organization need to start paying for it and reimbursing the United States for its expenses in hosting it.

In short, the federal government will begin to confine its activities to what they were ordained to do by "We the people," in our Constitution.

They'll be a lot of change in the works – huge and necessary restoration – but we'll work together as a nation in making it happen.

We Must!!!

Our Republic needs some life support!!!

And, yes .. these changes need to include those now famous entitlements .. Social Security, Medicare, and Medicaid. Those programs are not constitutional and need to be phased out as well.

Promises were made, and most importantly, money was taken from our fellow Americans for those programs. Somehow, we will need to put together a plan, or plans, that honor the promises that were made and to bring some return to the money that's been taken from people.

The truth be known, there have been an assortment of potential remedies and plans on how to fix this dilemma; but the bottom-line is that we need to look at this and come to some sort of adequate resolve that will be fair to all those American citizens involved (and please do note the specific and purposeful reference to "American citizens" - only American citizens).

I personally enjoy the plans that include taking the assets from those who continually robbed from these "funds", who repeatedly made themselves (and their friends) exempt from these Ponzi schemes, and who structured a host of sweetheart deals that very adequately takes care of themselves with money and benefits. Those folks being the past and present ones who have enabled this travesty – Congress and its ilk.

<u>They</u> .. have stolen from the people they were supposed to safeguard and represent. The long line of them are practiced thieves versus good stewards!

Albeit, we will have to explore a variety of solutions to this massive problem; but we also need to stop feeding it. There is absolutely no good reason American citizens in their mid-30's and under are having to continue paying into this government swindle – this government sponsored ponzi scheme.

I have no doubt that we can find workable solutions to all of the problems that we'll have to address as we move back into a federal government that follows the Constitution. Sacrifices will have to be made; but to simply continue to do what we've been doing will bring more serious calamity and ruin all opportunity for our posterity.

Remember .. we'll be using the Constitution as our guide; and, we'll have a lot of quality people working with us.

Let's get running!

We've got a lot of work to do!

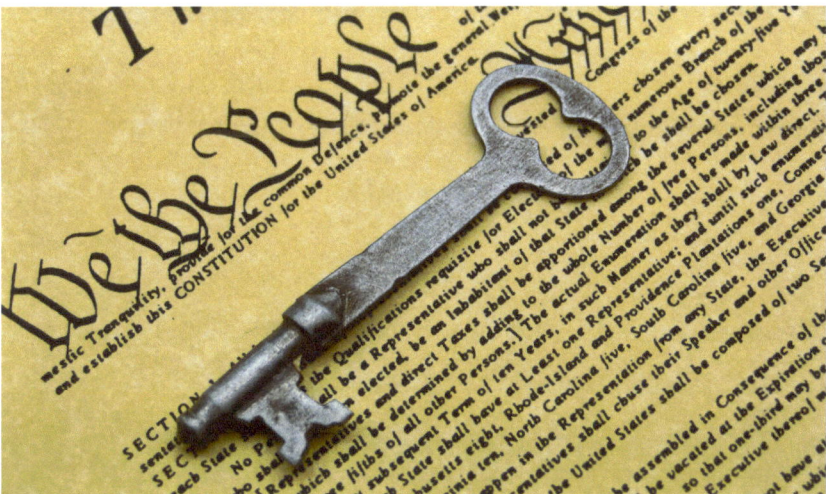

But What About Some of the Other Stuff?

The pomp and circumstance - the Wednesday night White House frat parties - the cool and exotic vacations?

Yeah. The cool stuff.

The golf games and luxury coach get-a-ways. The partying with the jet setters, the sports figures, the rock bands, the Holly-weirdos, and all that high roller fun stuff.

The wonderful trips that include all sorts of friends and family. The special "favors" for special folks and – shhhhhhhhh - the special "favors" offered in return - that, of course, we need to be quiet about.

"We gonna get in on all that stuff?"

There's been an ugly precedent set by a certain "party president" that seems to imply (and exhibit) that the "sky's the limit" for the king and his proverbial court.

That same "party president" likes to tout that so many of his ideas and plans are 'Paid For" by this or that.

Newsflash!

We are broke!!!

We are a country that has surpassed a debt load of 117 trillion dollars!!!

Nothing is paid for!!!

Let me repeat that .. NOTHING is paid for!!!

Our debt has finally gone beyond our entire national gross domestic product; and the fools sitting at the helm of this unfunded ship are showing no signs of slowing down with their spending plans.

"Oh, but let's scramble about and pass a "Balanced Budget Amendment"."

"That'll fix the problem, right?"

<u>No</u>! <u>Not at all</u>!

That will kick the can down the road again under the guise of doing something good for the Country. We'll continue to sink into debt further; but the helmsmen will have yet another piece of the Constitution that they can ignore.

A return to the federal government spending **<u>ONLY</u>** what is authorized in the Constitution for them to spend will be the single most effective remedy for our financial crisis!

The budget will be able to be balanced.

Debt will be able to be paid down – not increased through these fraudulent and never ending debt ceiling raises.

We are broke and this spending party needs to be over!

Let's look again at the wisdom of one of our Founders as he contemplated finances. Mr. Thomas Jefferson said, "The principle of spending money to be paid for by posterity, under the name of funding, is but **<u>swindling futurity on a large scale</u>**."

He also stated that, "To preserve our independence, we must not let our rulers load us with perpetual debt. We must make our election between economy and liberty, or profusion and servitude. I place economy among the first and most important of republican virtues, and **public debt as the greatest of the dangers** to be feared."

<u>Right on, Mr. Jefferson!!!</u>

We will not be party to the swindling of futurity on any scale. We will be very economic and behave in ways to support that concept.

There will be no Wednesday White House parties. Air Force One (and all the companion planes and equipment) will be used very sparingly and for business only when necessary.

An intense and thorough review and overhaul of the expenditures that go on in DC by all branches of government (including the Executive Branch) will be conducted and real world solutions and economic reforms will be implemented.

Many of these bureaucrats will be introduced to "Go-to-Meeting" instead of personal government jets and 1rst class plane tickets.

The notion of these "perks to the privileged" will be eliminated; and all branches will be adjusted so their activities <u>serve the people</u> – <u>not the people and their money serving them</u>.

Some simple and common sense changes in behavior, a sincere realignment of the focus of the duty, and a true interest to <u>serve the nation</u> will certainly lead us to economic savings.

I'd go so far as to say, at minimum, 20% of the expenses across the board in DC could be eliminated by the adjustment of some behaviors and practices .. and, it will be.

One of the duties of the President, for instance, is to receive Heads-of-State and foreign dignitaries. Let's go ahead and buy them lunch or a dinner when prudent; but we don't need to host parties for the Hollywood gang, Rappers, and other "special favored friends".

The nation's business needs to be conducted in the nation's office. Misuse of a privilege or of an expense account really is a crime (theft); and in the private sector, those who misuse and abuse their allotments are usually fired.

DC needs to get that message, too - once and for all.

It's easy to spend money when it belongs to someone else. Our leaders .. from top to bottom and on both sides of the aisle .. need to become honest and good stewards of our dollars; not self-serving thieves. Not charlatans who pile boundless amounts of debt upon us.

All operational expenditures of the federal government will be reviewed and adjusted to make sure Americans are getting the absolute best value and return for their dollars.

Amongst our first year goals will be to task every supervisor and/or manager to flex their management skills and discover ways for their operations to continue with budgets of 20% less.

Hopefully, they'll be worthy and able managers; because that's what their budgets will be – 20% less.

The average American family is being asked to do more with less .. now the government can learn to survive under that format, too.

No more, "Spend it, or lose it" mentality. The new mentality will be, "It ain't your money! Spend it as though it is yours 'cuz it just may be!".

So to speak to the "fun stuff", the pomp and circumstance, and so on .. you can expect a **huge** reduction in those expenses. While some of that "stuff" is necessary – that will be the deciding factor - is it really necessary?

If not, we save the money.

Vacations? Golf? Parties?

If we get the time.

Remember .. we're going to be very, very busy. If we have the time and want to vacation .. our vacations are on us. Like every other American citizen, we pay for our own fun stuff.

So .. let's get to work.
You're still running with me, right?

Is There Anything Else We Need to Highlight?

Yes!

Our task .. the return of the United States to Constitutional governance will be an encompassing and huge effort. As we've talked however, it is an absolutely necessary one.

There are people .. leaders .. organizations .. who seek to gain more power over America and the American people. Disgustingly, we have a president who claims to be a Constitutional expert that has announced his plans on asking Congress (yes .. that same Congress he usually ignores) for "more power to the executive".

Our Constitution has the schematic for the division of "power".

Our Constitution outlines the "power" delegated to the Executive.

Follow the schematic as it's outlined for God's sake!

This presidential, self-proclaimed Constitutional expert also recently said that our Founders put together a system that "slows him down and gets in the way." He just can't get everything done that he wants to do and quickly enough.

Thank God for the wisdom of our Founders!

Thank God for the plans He inspired our Founders with!

Dictators and tyrants operate extremely well in countries that have no plans or branches of government in place to limit or restrict their wants and desires.

Dictators and tyrants are usually pretty well convinced that they alone are capable of running things. They don't really need parliaments or Congresses.

Ask Castro. Ask Chavez. Ask Kim Jong III (or his son).

Ask any number of the dictators that show up at the U.N..

This Country <u>desperately</u> needs to restrain and limit the federal government – not give it more power! .. or, allow it to take it!

If the individual States want all kinds of programs, agencies, departments, and such; if their State Constitution allows for it all, if their citizens want it and they can pay for it .. have at it.

The 10th Amendment of the Constitution of the United States says, "The powers not delegated to the United States (the federal government) by the Constitution, nor prohibited by it to the States, are reserved to the States respectively, or to the people."

So indeed, .. States .. gear up to assume the duties that belong to you already; and be prepared to take on those that will be phased out from under the Federal umbrella that don't belong there anyway - providing you want them.

By the end of our first term, our goal would be that we are well on our way restoring our Federal Government to one our Founders would recognize and be proud of – one our citizens could be happy with and live free.

Amazingly (and disgustingly), we have a misguided Supreme Court Justice who has taken an oath to support and defend the Constitution of the United States; but when asked by a developing country creating one, she steered them in a whole different direction by saying, "I would not look at the U.S. Constitution ..".

Imagine that!

And this Supreme Court justice took an oath to uphold and defend the US Constitution.

How sincere was she with that oath?

Those that want to stay in power and continue to peddle their influence and buy votes will fight this restoration tooth and nail with their gaggle of helpers like this Justice.

We need to be resolute!!!

Our return to Constitutional Governance must begin!!!

The truth is that there will be some sacrifices that will have to be made by all. Changes will be implemented sensibly and with sensitivity. These shifts will be a process and will always be considerate of the human impact to our citizens.

Our work will be the result of many fine people – guided by our Constitution and moving in some very specific directions with the purposeful restoration of the Country as its complete focus.

Our goal is not to hurt anyone. On the contrary, our goal is to save this great Country and put it back on the path away from tyranny and towards freedom, opportunity of all sorts, and justice for all.

Our Constitution has been violated and ignored.

The golden goose has been choked.

The Statue of Liberty is on life support.

We can stay on the path we've been on and we will see America's demise and the world will be changed forever.

We will all suffer!!!

Or .. we can be courageous enough to seek that return to the "magic formula" that propelled this Country to magnificent heights and an enviable stature.

We can return to the plan for greatness that's brought by limiting and restraining governments and placing trust and faith in **"We, the people"**.

The final choice is really ours to make.

You and I are running on a platform that should encourage ..

"We, the people "

Let's get busy.

And To Highlight One More Thing

.. possibly the most important thing to highlight ..

According to the story, as our Founders grappled with the task of putting our Constitution together, they reached a dangerous crossroads in their discussions. Passions and tempers were running high and it appeared that the talks would completely break down and cease.

We were at the verge of not having the Constitution being created!

Ben Franklin, the oldest of the representatives at the convention, sensed the gravity of the moment and rose to address the gathering.

He said, "Mr. President: The small progress we've made after four or five weeks of close attendance and continual reasonings with each other – our different sentiments on almost every question, several of the last producing as many no's as ayes – is methinks a melancholy proof of the imperfection of the Human Understanding."

He went on, "We indeed seem to feel our own want of political wisdom, since we've been running in search of it. We have gone back to ancient history for models of government, and examined the different forms of those Republics which .. having been formed with the seeds of their own dissolution .. now no longer exist."

"And we have viewed Modern States all around Europe, but found none of their Constitutions suitable to our circumstances."

"In this situation of this Assembly groping as it were in the dark to find political truth, and scarce able to distinguish it when it is shown to us, .. how has it happened, Sir, that we have not hitherto once thought of humbly applying to the Father of Lights to illuminate our understandings?"

"In the beginning of the contest with Great Britain, when we were sensible of danger .. we had daily prayer in this room for Divine Protection .."

"Our prayers, Sir, we're heard, and they were graciously answered!!!"

"All of us who were engaged in the struggle must have observed <u>frequent</u> instances of a Superintending Providence in our favor."

"To that kind providence we owe this happy opportunity of consulting in peace on the means of establishing our future national felicity. And have we now forgotten that powerful friend? Or do we imagine that we no longer need His assistance."

"I have lived, Sir, a long time ... and the longer I live, the more convincing proofs I see of this truth – that God governs in the affairs of men."

"And if a sparrow cannot fall to the ground without His notice, is it probable that an empire can rise without His aid?"

"We have been assured, Sir, in the Sacred Writings that 'except the Lord build they labor in vain that build it'."

"I firmly believe this; and I also believe that without His concurring aid we shall succeed in this political building no better than the builders of Babel: We shall be divided by our little partial local interests; our projects will be confounded, and we ourselves shall become a reproach and a bye word down to future age."

"And what is worse, mankind may hereafter this unfortunate instance, despair of establishing governments by Human Wisdom, and leave it instead to chance, war, and conquest."

Mr. Franklin concluded with, "I therefore beg leave to move – that henceforth – prayers imploring the assistance of Heaven, and its blessings on our deliberations, .. be held in this Assembly every morning before we proceed to business, and that one or more of the Clergy of this City be requested to officiate in that service."

The delegates endorsed Mr. Franklin's appeal; and according to the story, prayer was added to their routine and significant progress was again made. The result .. our magnificent Constitution.

A Constitution that propelled this Country to new and unimaginable heights. A plan that was Divinely inspired that enabled men to govern themselves and live free.

Fast forward to today .. what have we done to our national recognition and connection with God?

Why have we allowed small segments of our society to push God and Godly things out of the picture?

Why have we allowed a phony notion of a "separation of church and state" to cause so much damage to us and create such destruction to our nation?

This insanity really must stop!

Just as Mr. Franklin reminded those early Patriots engaged in developing our Constitution to again ask for, and rely upon, God's good grace and blessings; we too, will ask the nation to join us in the inclusion of a loving and generous God to return to our daily lives and our national landscape.

A great nation did rise with His aid ..

With His aid again, a great nation may rise again!!!

If we leave out this all important dynamic.. God .. God in our Country .. our toils will likely be in vain; and our destruction will be the same as those of biblical Babel.

Our administration .. yours and mine .. will be certain to invite God into all we do – much like those early American Patriots and our Founders did as they went about and built this great nation.

We will be very mindful of Mr. Franklin's commentary and question, **"is it probable that an empire can rise without His aid?"**; and we will ask all Americans to be very mindful of that as well.

We'll ask all Americans to join us in the practice of the words of our very first President as he encouraged us when he said ..

".. it is the duty of all nations to acknowledge the providence of Almighty God, to obey His will, to be

grateful for His benefits, and humbly implore His protection and favour ..".

I'm still running. How 'bout you?

With God's good grace .. we'll do superbly.

The End Game

"So, this business of running for president is serious stuff, isn't it?"

More serious than what may appear on the surface. Putting the proverbial chicken in every pot really isn't the mission or purpose of government, is it? Making everybody happy at the end of the day isn't really where it's at, is it?

For a long time now, folks that want to be in power and control have tried to appeal to those base desires. They have enjoyed differing measures of success along the way; and the attitudes of many have been changed immensely at the same time.

John Kennedy in the 60's said, "Ask not what your Country can do for you ...".

Politicians of today talk of what they'll give you and how they'll make your life easier and almost problem free. Look at the gaggle of goons that drool over those "terrific" Occupy Wall Streeters – God Bless 'em, Nancy, .. right (???).

Has a new sense been birthed in America? A new sense that aligns with this philosophy ...

"Hate the man who is better off than you are. Never .. under any circumstances .. admit that his success may be due to his own efforts, or to the productive contribution he has made to the whole community. Always attribute his success to the exploitation, the cheating, the more or less open robbery of others. Never

.. under any circumstances .. admit that your own failure may be owing to your own weakness; or that the failure of anyone else may be due to his own defects .. his own laziness, his own incompetence, his own improvidence, or his own stupidity."

I would pray that that is not a new and acceptable sense for any American. It has the ability to destroy America and Americans. Sadly, in many cases however, it appears that it may be a newer and growing "sense".

This philosophy, "Hate the man who is better off than you ...", is exactly how an American economist, Henry Hazlitt (1894-1993), responded when asked about Karl Marx and Marxism.

His answer was, **"The whole gospel of Karl Marx can be summed up in a single sentence: Hate the man who is better off than you are."**

Breathtaking, ay.

Breathtaking because isn't that what's really behind this class warfare nonsense we hear from even many in "leadership" roles – "leadership" positions.

The philosophy of Marx being promoted here in America – the Land of the Free .. Home of the Brave – by many of our very own elected leaders. Those same leaders who take an oath to support and defend the Constitution for the United States.

Talk about delusional and misguided.

Our message to America .. to Americans .. needs to be much more encouraging and much more truthful than this selfish, greedy, self-serving, and class warfare tripe.

Our message needs to include a call to all to be very mindful of all the wonderful things we have to be grateful for in this Country. We have been, and truly still are, very blessed in this country. The U.S. is the world's most envied nation. We need to be certain that we are very mindful of a true sense of gratitude for all we've been blessed with.

We need to allow that sense of gratitude to swell and enrich our Spiritual life – individually and nationally.

If we can develop an individual and national sense that says we're grateful for all we have, we can avoid the disappointment and complaining that comes with the whining about what we don't have.

We need to allow this renewed grasp on gratitude affirm our belief in a loving and generous God. A God who will bless, grace, strengthen, and guide His Faithful. A God who will reward His faithful in Godly ways. A God who will help us heal our nation and recover well.

Our message to the nation must always embrace God!!!

Remember again, the words of our very first President when he said,

".. it is the duty of all nations to acknowledge the providence of Almighty God, to obey His will, to be grateful for His benefits, and humbly implore His protection and favour .."

After all, we did have another president who talked about "words having meaning – they must mean something", he said.

Imagine living in a country that brings life to General George Washington's words.

"Almighty God" .. "Divine Providence" .. "Father of Lights"

We couldn't ask for a better Head of State!!!

And to Him, I'd gladly yield that top spot. With His aid, we all can manage better; but put Him at the head of the table and get ready for unimaginable results!

"But what about our run for the presidency?" you might ask.

We'll run alright.

We just may not go to Washington or do all those campaigning gigs. Our names may not appear on any of the ballots. They'll likely not be any presidential portraits painted of us or an aircraft carrier named after us.

But ... we'll run.

Hopefully, our presence will be felt everywhere that there is an American flag flying.

With God's good grace, we may make a positive imprint upon our fellow citizens and attract their attention towards helping our nation during its troubled times.

Our ideas might resonate wherever and whenever there's a discussion involving America; and ideally, folks may seek to search out and learn the wisdom of our Founders.

With our encouragement, every American maybe will become a sincere and patriotic ambassador for our Country and know what it stands for and what it represents.

If we can eagerly accept the grand opportunity of being an American, then we need to be responsible enough to always "run for President" ... to always strive to be the best example of what America has to offer.

We need to be engaged in our Country and we need to keep our eyes on those steering this ship-of-state. It's been said that, "The price of freedom is eternal vigilance."

That begs the question, "How vigilant am I being towards the preservation of this beacon of freedom and liberty in the world?"

So, yes .. we'll run.

Every day we'll run. Every day we'll be vigilant. Every day we'll be alert to violations against our Constitution and Country and respond to them accordingly. Every day we'll engage in some display of patriotism and encourage others to do the same. Every day we can pray for our Country's well being, our fellow citizens, and mankind.

Every day we can be "President".

Every day we should act as if we were.

"We the people," after all, are the bosses!

Have no misgivings whatsoever. Our Country is under attack. Our Country and all that it represents is being assaulted daily. Very subtle attacks; but repetitive and caustic attacks. Attacks that are being perpetrated even by those who claim to have our best interests in mind.

<u>We all need to become Presidents</u>!!!

You've likely noticed that I've been inviting you all along!!!

Learn the truthful history of your Country. Read the Founding Documents – the Declaration of Independence and Constitution. Study the accurate accountings of our Founders and their writings. Be proud of your Country and its Heritage .. there's much to be proud of.

Connect with others who are active in the Country's well being. Continue to learn and grow. Don't be afraid to add your voice and ideas to the mix. Cherish what you have here in America – it wasn't easily gotten.

Allow no one to diminish it.

<u>So .. Yes! Run for President with me .. please</u>!!!

Our platform will be pretty simple and unchanging ..

Include God in our lives.

Include God in our national existence and landscape.

Return to Constitutional Governance.

May God Bless America!!!

God Bless Our Troops and Veterans!!!

May God Bless Each and Every One of You!!!

About the Author

John is a patriotic American from Minnesota and the Founding Director of The 56 Club - an organization founded in the spirit of the 56 Signers of the Declaration of Independence.

His father was a career Navy man; and because of that, the family was reasonably traveled – spending several years living in the country of Japan during the mid and late '50's.

"My youthful exposure to our military services – coupled with the opportunity to travel to other countries even – all have deeply ingrained into me a sincere love for this Country and for those who serve it and help to make it great."

"I feel deeply blessed and fortunate to have been born into the greatest Country ever known to man; and would be very pleased if I could be even a small part in reminding people of the greatness of our Country and how blessed we are to be Americans!"

"Our Founders and the early Patriots were always concerned about posterity. I want to do my part in helping to insure a great America for the generations yet to come!"

"May God Bless us all .. and America!!!"

John can be contacted through The 56 Club website at:

www.the56club.com

or by mail at PO Box 21241, St Paul, MN 55121

Acknowledgements and Credits

There are numerous acknowledgements that need to be made to honor the many resources that went into the creation of this work.

First and foremost, tremendous honor and thanks must go to the collection of our Founders and early Patriots that gave so much of their beings and existence so that we could live in the greatest experiment in liberty and freedom ever .. and in the whole wide world.

Next, to the many sources of learning that helped to mold this work. The Heritage Foundation, the National Center for Constitutional Studies and their banner seminar, "The Making of America", the "Patriot Post", Hillsdale College and their "Imprimus" publication, David Barton's "WallBuilders" organization, and many, many others.

To those great Americans who so frequently encourage and direct folks to the wisdom and direction found in our Founding Documents .. Rush Limbaugh, Sean Hannity, and Mark Levin amongst so many others.

Thanks for being such a big part of this journey!

And specific credit to the illustration providers of the art work appearing herein .. CanStock Photo: eagle with flag - csp0068869lisafx, flag with fireworks - csp1857987 sarah5, Constitution with flag - csp0160792webking, and Constitution with key - cssp0897856rsugden - the Constitution is the key.

Many, many heartfelt thanks to all!

www.ingramcontent.com/pod-product-compliance
Lightning Source LLC
Chambersburg PA
CBHW041214270326

41930CB00001B/9